TEST!

COLLECT AND DOCUMENT DATA

Emma Carlson Berne

PowerKiDS press

Published in 2015 by The Rosen Publishing Group, Inc.
29 East 21st Street, New York, NY 10010

First Edition

Editor: Jennifer Way
Book Design: Kate Vlachos
Photo Research: Katie Stryker

Photo Credits: Cover oliveromg/Shutterstock.com; pp. 4–5 Sam DCruz/Shutterstock.com; pp. 6, 10, 12, 13, 15, 17, 18, 22 iStockphoto/Thinkstock; p. 7 Kenishirotie/Shutterstock.com; p. 8 Fuse/Thinkstock; p. 9 Zurijeta/Shutterstock.com; p. 11 Hemera/Thinkstock; p. 14 Gary John Norman/Iconica/Getty Images; p. 16 Marilyn Nieves/E+/Getty Images; p. 19 Peter Cade/Iconica/Getty Images; p. 20 Tim Platt/Iconica/Getty Images; p. 21 Steven Puetzer/Photographer's Choice RF/Getty Images.

Library of Congress Cataloging-in-Publication Data

Berne, Emma Carlson.
 Test! : collect and document data / by Emma Carlson Berne. — First edition.
     pages cm. — (The scientific method in action)
 Includes index.
 ISBN 978-1-4777-2928-1 (library) — ISBN 978-1-4777-3016-4 (pbk.) — ISBN 978-1-4777-3087-4 (6-pack)
 1. Science—Methodology—Juvenile literature. I. Title.
 Q175.2.B475 2015
 507.2′4—dc23
                                    2013025977

Manufactured in the United States of America

CPSIA Compliance Information: Batch #WS14PK5: For Further Information contact Rosen Publishing, New York, New York at 1-800-237-9932

CONTENTS

THE SCIENTIFIC METHOD

Scientists ask questions and try to find answers about why things happen in our world. Some scientists work in a **laboratory**. Others work outside the lab in places like the ocean or at the South Pole.

Scientists need to be very careful when they study how and why things happen. This is why they use a

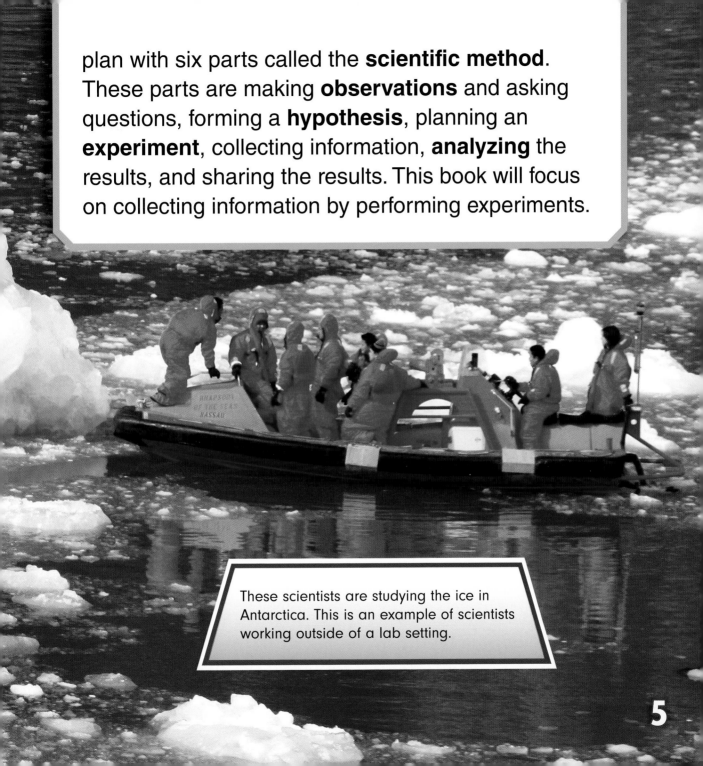

plan with six parts called the **scientific method**. These parts are making **observations** and asking questions, forming a **hypothesis**, planning an **experiment**, collecting information, **analyzing** the results, and sharing the results. This book will focus on collecting information by performing experiments.

These scientists are studying the ice in Antarctica. This is an example of scientists working outside of a lab setting.

READY, SET, EXPERIMENT!

When you walk through a garden, you may notice that the same plants look healthier in sunny areas than they do in shady areas. You may form a hypothesis based on this observation.

Before you perform your experiment, you should have already formed a hypothesis. For example, your hypothesis might be that plants will grow faster when there is plenty of sunlight than when they get less sunlight. You will test your hypothesis by growing plants under different sunlight conditions.

Don't forget that your experiment needs a **control** and a **variable**. The control is the part of the experiment that stays the same. The variable is the part of the experiment that changes. You will collect **data** throughout your experiment. Then, at the end, this data will help you figure out if you have proved or disproved your hypothesis.

For your experiment growing plants, you will change only one condition. This changed condition is the variable.

GETTING PREPARED

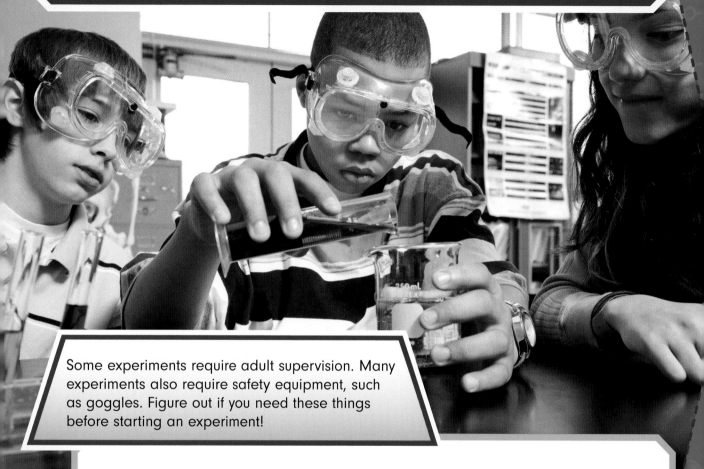

Some experiments require adult supervision. Many experiments also require safety equipment, such as goggles. Figure out if you need these things before starting an experiment!

Now it is time to get ready for your experiment! First, gather the supplies you will use in your experiment, including the tools to record your data. Data is the information you get from your experiment. In the plant experiment, this would include the hours of daily sunlight each plant received. It would also include the height each plant reached.

Depending on your experiment, you might need a pen, paper, a ruler, a stopwatch, a measuring beaker, a thermometer, or even a camera to record your data. You will need these data-recording items in addition to the items you need to run the experiment.

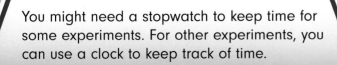

You might need a stopwatch to keep time for some experiments. For other experiments, you can use a clock to keep track of time.

RUNNING THE CONTROL

To begin your experiment, first run your control. For example, for your plant experiment, give your plant the same amount of light every day. Note the other conditions, such as how much water you give the plant each day and how tall the plant is. Write down what the plant looks like. Even better, take a photograph!

It is a good idea to measure the water you give to the plants in your experiment. That way you can give all of the plants in your experiment the same amount of water each day.

Take notes on everything you do for your control plant. Write down all the data carefully.

Record your observations over a period of time. After that time period has passed, look at your results. How much taller is the plant? Are there more leaves? Is the plant the same color? Take another picture of your plant, and compare it to your first picture.

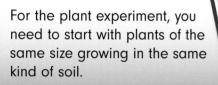

For the plant experiment, you need to start with plants of the same size growing in the same kind of soil.

Now you are ready to test your variable. You will compare these results with the results of your control. Use exactly the same conditions that you used for the control. For instance, choose a plant of the same type and size as your control plant. Photograph and record all of the same information you recorded about the control plant. Now, instead of putting the plant in a sunny windowsill, keep it away from sunlight.

Record all the data exactly as you did with your control. You will use these results later to determine if your hypothesis was correct.

You might think about using a special plant-growing light in your experiment. This will allow you to be more accurate with the hours of light your plants get.

REPEAT THE EXPERIMENT

You might think that after you have run your control and your variable, you are done with your experiment. You're not, though!

Scientists always repeat their experiments. When you do this, you use the same materials under the

Record your data each time you run your experiment. This will help you see if you have made any mistakes in your experiment.

If your experiment involves keeping plants on a certain windowsill, do not move them! This is a change that could affect your results.

same conditions and record the data each time. Then, make sure your results are the same as they were the first time you ran the experiment. When you do this, you make sure that you did not make a mistake during the experiment, such as giving the plants different amounts of water.

CHECK YOUR WORK

You can use a computer to write up your notes. This can make it easier to check your work.

You've run your experiment several times. You've recorded the data for your control and your variable. Now it is time to check your work. Carefully look over all of your notes. Is all of the information you recorded complete? Are you missing any important information?

You also want to note anything unusual that might have happened during the experiment. Did your cat chew on one of the plants' leaves? Write that down. Note any surprise or unexpected results. You may not know why you got those results, but you can investigate later when you analyze your data.

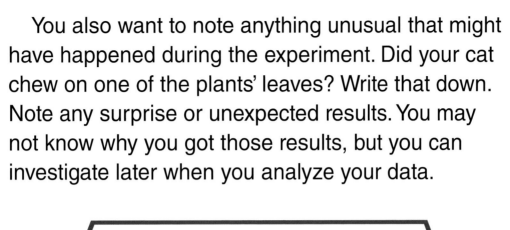

Did you keep your plants outside during your experiment? If so, make sure to note any weather changes that could have affected your results.

MAKING OBSERVATIONS

Now it is time to write up your observations. Think about what happened in your experiment. Look at your data, your notes, and your photographs and write down anything interesting you see. For example, you might write, "I have observed that the plant given 8 hours of sunlight per day grew .5 inch (1.27 cm) and gained two

Observations are anything you can see. When you write your observations, make them complete sentences.

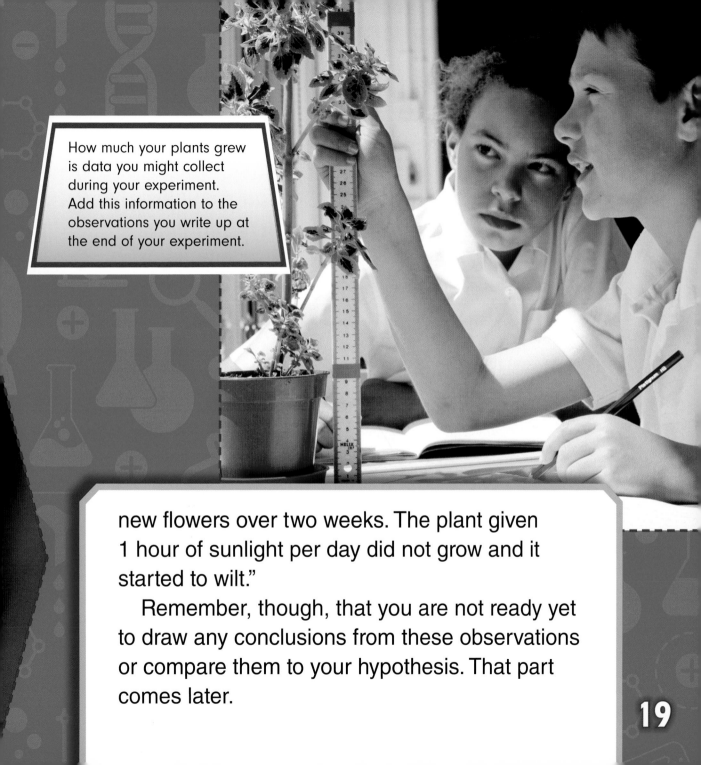

How much your plants grew is data you might collect during your experiment. Add this information to the observations you write up at the end of your experiment.

new flowers over two weeks. The plant given 1 hour of sunlight per day did not grow and it started to wilt."

Remember, though, that you are not ready yet to draw any conclusions from these observations or compare them to your hypothesis. That part comes later.

THINKING VISUALLY

When you write up your data, you can also make it into graphic organizers, such as charts and graphs. Seeing your data laid out **visually** can help you better understand the results.

You can draw a chart or a graph with pens or markers. You can also use a computer to make

Graphic organizers make information easier to understand. These people have made a pie chart on the computer.

A pie chart is best if your data is in the form of percentages. A bar graph is good at showing the differences between times or amounts. A line graph is great at showing changes over a span of time.

You could make graphic organizers using markers. However, you will need to do it carefully or they will not be accurate.

neater, more accurate, and easier to read graphic organizers. Ask your teacher or your school librarian to show you the programs that you can use. Once you have all of your data collected and organized, you are ready to analyze it to see if your hypothesis was correct.

ACCURATE DATA

Creating a repeatable experiment is important in making scientific discoveries, but so is collecting and recording data accurately. In 1999, scientists at the Lawrence Berkeley National Laboratory thought they had discovered something new about **atoms**. They were very excited they had proved their hypothesis. It turned out that their data was inaccurate, though. The scientists had to **retract** their findings.

Running an experiment is one of the most important and difficult parts of the scientific method. Making sure your data is accurate is essential.

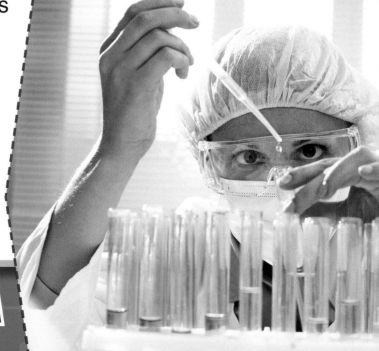

Scientists measure everything very carefully when they run experiments. Even a small mistake can lead to incorrect results.

GLOSSARY

analyzing (A-nuh-lyz-ing) Examining something carefully and thinking about what it means.

atoms (A-temz) The smallest parts of elements.

control (kun-TROHL) The standard of an experiment that produces what is expected for a result.

data (DAY-tuh) Facts.

experiment (ik-SPER-uh-ment) A test done on something to learn more about it.

hypothesis (hy-PAH-theh-ses) Something that is suggested to be true for the purpose of an experiment or argument.

laboratory (LA-bruh-tor-ee) A room in which scientists do tests.

observations (ahb-ser-VAY-shunz) Things that are seen or noticed.

retract (rih-TRAKT) To take back.

scientific method (sy-en-TIH-fik MEH-thud) The system of running experiments in science.

variable (VER-ee-uh-bul) An element in an experiment that may be changed.

visually (VIH-zhuh-wul-ee) Shown through a piece of illustrative material, such as a photo, graph, or diagram.

INDEX

WEBSITES

Due to the changing nature of Internet links, PowerKids Press has developed an online list of websites related to the subject of this book. This site is updated regularly. Please use this link to access the list:
www.powerkidslinks.com/smia/test/